You Will Remember Me

You Will Remember Me

ekphrastic poems

by

Barbara Lydecker Crane

WORD GALAXY PRESS
An imprint of Able Muse Press

Word Galaxy Press

www.wordgalaxy.com

Printed in the United States of America

Library of Congress Cataloging-in-Publication Data

Names: Crane, Barbara Lydecker, 1948- author.
Title: You will remember me / poems by Barbara Lydecker Crane.
Description: San Jose, CA : Word Galaxy Press, 2023.
Identifiers: LCCN 2022028038 (print) | LCCN 2022028039 (ebook) | ISBN
    9781773491264 (paperback) | ISBN 9781773491271 (ebook)
Subjects: LCSH: Painting--Poetry. | LCGFT: Ekphrastic poetry.
Classification: LCC PS3603.R378 Y68 2022 (print) | LCC PS3603.R378 (ebook) |
    DDC 811/.6--dc23/eng/20220614
LC record available at https://lccn.loc.gov/2022028038
LC ebook record available at https://lccn.loc.gov/2022028039

Cover image: *Her Artpreciation* by Alexander Pepple
   (with *Art Time* by Sofya Borboris and *Self-Portrait from L'ile Saint Louis* by Henri Rousseau)

Cover & book design by Alexander Pepple

Word Galaxy Press is an imprint of Able Muse Press—at
www.ablemusepress.com

Word Galaxy Press
467 Saratoga Avenue #602
San Jose, CA 95129

Acknowledgments

Grateful acknowledgment is made to the editors of the following publications in which these poems, some in earlier versions, first appeared:

Able Muse: "The Empty Lap of Luxury"

Alabama Literary Review: "Imagining Caleb," "Marie de Valengin," and "Rivals"

Better than Starbucks: "Out of Sight"

Blue Unicorn: "Arrangement, with Mother" (as "My Arrangement with Mother") and "Before the Revolution"

The Ekphrastic Review: "Afresh," "After Influenza," "Arrangements," "The Blue Hour," "Brood" (as "House of Cards"), "Caprice for the King," "A Certain Symmetry" (finalist for the Women Artist Award), "Devotion," "I Am What God Has Made Me" (as "Self-Portrait at Twenty-Eight"), "On My Terms," "Painting Henry," and "Reflection" (nominated for a Pushcart Prize)

Gyroscope Review: "Self-Portrait at a Torture Wheel"

Innisfree Poetry Journal: "Charming Nelly" (as "May Afternoons"), "Girl with a Turban," "Incandescence," "My Other Life," and "To My Art Students"

The Lyric: "Presenting Myself"

Maria W. Faust Sonnet Contest: "Black Bird" (Laureate's Choice Award)

Mezzo Cammin: "The Desperate Man" and "She Winds a Chain around Her Finger"

Montreal Review: "Lifelines," "Stanislawa's Hair Is Brushed and Bowed," "Traitor" (as "Portrait of Zamor"), and "When I Was Young"

The Orchards: "My Present"

Pulsebeat Poetry Journal: "The Miniaturist"

Rattle: "Mother and Child" (finalist for the Rattle Poetry Prize) and "You Will Remember Me"

The Road Not Taken: "Unspoken" (as featured poem)

Sparks of Calliope: "Little Bird" and "On the Island"

Snakeskin: "Boterismo" and "Miss Moore No More"

THINK: a Journal of Poetry, Fiction, and Essays: "Close-Up," "My Brother with the Same Name," "No Angels," and "Scandal" (as "Madame X")

Valparaiso Poetry Review: "The Opera Box"

My gratitude goes to the sponsors of the following contests, in which recognition did not include publication of these poems:

Soul-Making Keats Literary Competition, Sonnet Category: first prize, "My Other Life"; honorable mention, "Brood" (as "House of Cards")

Helen Schaible Sonnet Contest, Traditional Sonnets: second prize, "Scandal" (as "Madame X")

Verbatim quotes from the artist featured in a given poem are presented in italics and are acknowledged as such in "Notes," beginning on page 71, which also provide directions for locating the corresponding artwork online if it's not included with the poem. (Italics are also used for emphasis, for names of artworks, and for foreign words.)

The epigraph for each poem presents the following information in the order listed: the title of the painting, the date it was painted, the name of the artist, the dates of the artist's life, and the place where the painting was created. If the artist's country of birth differs from that of the painting's creation, the former is provided before the birth date.

Contents

You Will Remember Me

You Will Remember Me

Marie de Valengin

Portrait of a Lady, circa 1460
Rogier van der Weyden (circa 1400–1464), Brussels

Something brewed beneath her cool remove
when she sat down and held her body still
as I began to paint. "Père won't approve,"
she murmured, tightly clasping hands. "What will
my father do? I want to be a nun."
With that, she dipped her head as if in prayer.
Her father, duke of Burgundy, isn't one
to pass the chance for an amorous affair.
Outside of marriage he has sired plenty;
Marie is one. At court he's schooled her well
and cossets her with jewels. But now, at twenty,
she fears her future as a demoiselle—
a cunning figure paired with charming face.
I've seen her dodge her father's fond embrace.

A Painting for Private Devotion

Madonna with Sleeping Child, circa 1465
Andrea Mantegna (1431–1506), Mantua, Italy

She's very young and almost real. In shadowed
light she holds with tenderness and care
the swaddled newborn baby sleeping there
against her breast. She's lovely and aglow
in pensive gaze. No halo need adorn.
The mother's hands support the holy child;
she rests her cheek upon his head, beguiled,
but in her eyes there's sorrow to be borne.

It's humanism that I wish to bring.
Let flesh and blood rekindle all my paints,
and let my brushstrokes echo sitters' breath.
I'm not alone to feel this welling spring
of wanting to depict not only saints,
but every life that shines until its death.

Model of a Saint

St. Sebastian, 1474
Sandro Botticelli (1445–1510), Florence

I paid this young man handsomely to pose.
I knew his striking, slim physique and height
would well display the raft of bloodless arrows
piercing him, recasting one saint's plight:
Saint Sebastian was martyred, lashed to a tree,
stripped (I draped a cloth around these hips),
shot with arrows, and left for dead. I see
my model differently. I paint his lips
and eyes in languid gaze, without a hint
of anguish: cared for, this man knows he'll live.
I'm cared for by my art and will not stint
in that devotion. I vow never to give
myself away to the burden of a wife.
Art provides the passions of my life.

His Latest Mistress

Lady with an Ermine, 1489–1490
Leonardo da Vinci (1452–1519), Milan

I paint Cecilia, fair and just sixteen,
plucked by my lustful patron, the duke of Milan.
For many years his courtiers have seen
his women come and go. This girl has gone
four months to bearing him another child.
The lively girl confides she plays the flute
and writes poems; no wonder she's beguiled
the duke. At times I'd like to be that brute.
I jabber on to hide my blush, recite
how I have purchased several caged birds
only to release them, in my study of flight.
Cecilia faintly smiles at my words
and strokes her silken ermine. Her gaze turns
toward distant music; she holds the pose, but yearns.

I Am What God Has Made Me

Self-Portrait at Twenty-Eight, 1500
Albrecht Dürer (1471–1528), Nuremberg

No, the archetype's not lost on me.
One hand upraised to heart as if to bless—
my frontal pose, symmetrical and pious—
is seen by some as that of Christ Almighty.
It's true I am endowed with special power
as an artist. I've kept this for myself;
my portrait rests upon my topmost shelf,
reminding me that every trumpet flower,
fluted lily, man, and mandolin
all sing the clear perfection of their maker.
I paint myself to be an image breaker
this new century. Remorse, chagrin,
humility, I do not choose to know.
My God creates above and I below.

Rivals

Self-Portrait, circa 1504–1506
Raphael (1483–1520), Urbino, Italy

I hope my languid eyes will draw your gaze
to my simple composition of chestnut, umber,
and black; against the dark my pale flesh plays
in subtle shadows. There's nothing to encumber
or embellish my likeness or my skill.
I'm only twenty-three, and have already
been awarded large commissions that fill
my pockets. And to fill my bed, a steady
stream of women. I'm nearly sure I've more
of them than he, whose name I will not say.
How well he sculpts and paints, I can't ignore—
so well, I wish he'd come undone today.
David, a marvel, lives and breathes in stone—
as I do here in paint. We stand alone.

Painting Henry

Henry VIII, 1540
Hans Holbein the Younger (Germany, circa 1497–1543)
Hampton Court, England

To feed my family, I paint his girth again
(such privilege at court I can't evade).
King Henry's doublet could enfold three men
inside its mink and glinting gold brocade.
I draped a band of jewels around his chest;
together with the slope of his plumed hat,
it makes a hint of halo—my private jest
and public gibe at this colossal rat.
Although I've made his royal raiment glow,
I've not adorned the plunder of his face:
his tiny mouth, his cheeks like risen dough,
his weasel eyes. And though I know my place
and bow to most caprices and commands,
I won't enlarge his most unmanly hands.

The Old Commander

Portrait of Hosokawa Takakuni, 1543
Kanō Motonobu (1476–1559), Kyoto

The old commander thought my brushwork fine—
remarking on my skill, my flowing line.
I paint his brown kimono's waves and folds
to ripple round and down the man. He holds
his hands together with upward-facing palms
as if in need of blessing, food, or alms.
He orders that his face be painted plain,
as if age lines were washed away by rain.
His gaze is steady and his mouth is set.
His mind might brim with pride or with regret:
he tersely relates the murder by his brother
and then he murmurs, "I arranged another,
avenging our dead father." Honor, respect,
remorse, and sorrow are rivers that connect.

She Winds a Chain around Her Finger

Portrait of a Lady, 1551
Catharina van Hemessen (1528–circa 1587), Antwerp

This woman casts a shadow; she looks real,
so real that one imagines she could walk
out from the picture frame. We'd hear her talk
about her pending union—the appeal
of having children, a respected place
in Flemish life—but, too, of reining in
herself, obeisance to that next of kin.
Of modest means, without a comely face,
this woman faced the choice that I would, too.
At twenty-six I looked at my position:
although my art had earned me recognition,
I put aside my paints and I withdrew
to wed. What made me close the door to fame
was fervent hope for children. They never came.

The Miniaturist

Portrait of Elizabeth I, circa 1565
Levina Teerlinc (Belgium, circa 1510–1576), London

For thirty years I've lived and thrived at court
through tact and artistry. King Henry paid
me forty pounds per annum, which by report
was more than court painter Holbein made.
How hard he worked—aloof, apart from wife
and children, striving to please the royal eyes.
My family lives with me, which makes my life
the richer. But riches cannot bar surprise—
as when the plague comes seeping through the door.
It came for poor Holbein. My silent prayers
preserve my days; pray God I'm granted more.
I paint our fair young queen with fine brush hairs
and sharpened quills, to limn a lively face
that dwells within its frame of earthly space.

Arrangements

Self-Portrait at the Clavichord with a Servant, 1577
Lavinia Fontana (1552–1614), Bologna

Bemoaning me unwed at twenty-five,
my needy father thought my art a draw,
a sort of future dowry. He contrived
how I'd impress my future father-in-law:
I'd paint myself arrayed in lace and satin
at the clavichord (a skill I cannot claim);
I spoke my virtue and smattering of Latin
with *virginem* inscribed beside my name.
My portrait impressed; the fathers did decide
I'd wed a man I'd never met. My Gian
began assisting me at work. His pride
survived the gossip, as did his jaunty grin.
"*Evirato*," he knew the neighbors said—
eleven babies put that barb to bed.

---

virginem (Latin): virgin
evirato (Italian): emasculated

Caprice for the King

Rudolph II of Hapsburg as Vertumnus, circa 1590
Giuseppe Arcimboldo (circa 1527–1593), Milan

King Rudolph chortles at my painted jest:
his radish rabbit teeth, his pea-green pods
for eyelids, his vegetally muscled chest.
I dubbed him *Vertumnus*, the Roman god
of metamorphoses and growing things.
Rare plants, astrology, and alchemy
delight Rudolph more than statecraft; the king
collects odd artwork with vitality.
Turning up in turnip, artichoke,
cabbage, apples, leeks, and spikes of grain,
he sees he is grotesque—in part a joke—
but too, a novel god. The king's domain
in Europe has grown to growing crops? I know
that painters profit when regal egos grow.

No Angels

Death of the Virgin, 1605–1606
Caravaggio (1571–1610), Rome

The Virgin Mary here is lying dead;
her body's not ascending out of sleep.
No angels herald her from overhead,
no holy symbols, save for one I keep—
her halo, that faint sliver. She wears a plain
red dress; her hair's askew; her feet are bare.
My patron sputters that this is profane,
beyond the bounds of what is doctrinaire.
My subject's all too real because I give her
the face and body of a prostitute
I knew who perished in the Tiber River.
Now she and I are both in disrepute:
my patron knew the woman, too. Ironic—
I've made the whore a virgin, and iconic.

The Poem I Tucked into the Frame

Double Portrait of Husband and Wife with Tulip, Bulb, and Shells, 1609
Michiel Janszoon van Mierevelt (1567–1641), Delft, Netherlands

Christina, my beloved wife, has died
too young, at thirty-nine. I paint today
from memory: she seems to sit beside
me now. Her gaze is soft, her ruff is gray,
her dress blends into darkness that surrounds.
She's part an apparition, come to grace
my life as if she'd risen from the ground.
She kept my art accounts and kept our place
agleam, with tulips brightening our tables
every April. In my hands I hold
a tulip and a bulb. The bulb enables
bloom; all through the numbing months of cold
an inner spark will slumber until spring.
Life encircles like a wedding ring.

Self-Portrait at a Torture Wheel

Self-Portrait as St. Catherine of Alexandria, circa 1615–1617
Artemisia Gentileschi (1593–circa 1654), Rome

Saint Catherine did survive the torture wheel,
because that wood-and-iron horror shattered
before its spikes could shred her skin. I feel
such pain when I remember my grim matter—
thumbscrews pressed to test my truth that Tassi,
my painting tutor, raped me at eighteen.
I prayed he'd hang in that morass. He,
found guilty and banished from Rome, still is seen
to lurk about. But I refuse to cower.
My sales are brisk; I paint my works with grace
and call on martyrdom as hidden power.
I paint a calm resolve into my face
while weighing my emotions and their uses . . .
to crown with haloes or to call for nooses.

Presenting Myself

Self-Portrait, circa 1630
Judith Leyster (1609–1660), Haarlem, Netherlands

This was my presentation to the Guild;
it never had admitted a female painter.
I sought to look at once relaxed and skilled
as I leaned back and smiled, but none the fainter
to have been born a woman. My lace ruff
was starched, my bodice plain (one hint of breast).
With grace I held my finest sable brush
and made my gaze look soft but self-possessed.
The fiddler I was painting with his bow
lightened up my portrait with bright notes.
I only showed the half of what I know
to the Haarlem Guild judges, those old goats.
They saw me here impeccably arrayed,
and just like that, the judges' votes were swayed.

What I Tell Myself

Self-Portrait, 1640
Jan Miense Molenaer (circa 1610–1668), Amsterdam

I feel not one but several decades older
than Judith was when painting her self-portrait.
A human skull makes my work somber, bolder—
of greater gravitas, I would purport—
in umber, gray, and black. My furrowed brow
is deeply shadowed over open books.
Despite the worries clouding my head now,
I still take pride in the style of my looks.
My hat with feathered plumes (the latest fashion)
and this expensive silver satin cloak
have nearly doubled debts from drink and passion,
as noted in this ledger. I am broke
but working hard, and surely sales will grow.
I'll hide the ledger. Judith won't yet know.

Note: Molenaer married Judith Leyster in 1636.

What Remains

Self-Portrait, 1658
Rembrandt van Rijn (1606–1669), Amsterdam

When debt overran me, my handsome, large
house was handed to the highest bidder.
That was pain enough, but the court took charge
of every one of my collections. Consider
my losses: art (even Greek and Roman),
weapons, armor, musical instruments. . . .
But a true connoisseur cannot be broken.
I will collect again, by increments.
A precious few possessions I have kept.
I'm wrapped in my ennobling cloak of fur
and golden satin robe; I grip the scepter
of my artist's stick. You must concur:
I'm still the king of painting dark and light.
I've not relinquished that, my artist's might.

Girl with a Turban

Girl with a Pearl Earring, circa 1665
Johannes Vermeer (1632–1675), Delft, Netherlands

I had this daughter pose. She was eleven
or twelve, and pleased to skirt her chores that day
as second mother to our other seven.
Paintings of exotic women pay
(and every grocer knows I'm short of cash),
and so I dressed Maria in a gold
coat and wrapped two lengths of silken sash
around her head in turban style; each fold
gleamed when I turned her head to catch the light.
To innocence I added some allure:
I had her lick and part her lips, not quite
prepared to speak. Enticing yet demure.
Watching me with liquid eyes, she shows
a wary longing for all she almost knows.

The Empty Lap of Luxury

Mr. and Mrs. Andrews, circa 1750
Thomas Gainsborough (1727–1788), Suffolk, England

It started well enough. My father owed
a debt to hers, and so I said I'd paint
this pair. They posed on land that was bestowed
on them—three thousand fertile acres. A faint
disdain dimmed her eyes and chilled her smile
at landless me. She shimmered in her gown
beside her rumpled hunter husband while
I painted this unspoken dressing-down.
The gunpowder pouch that dangled off her chap
became a limp but sporting specimen.
To fill in Mrs. Andrews' empty lap,
they asked for flowers. I would not give in:
a fresh-killed pheasant, I insisted. Deadlock.
A shame she wouldn't hold a lifeless cock.

Royall Treatment

Mary and Elizabeth Royall, circa 1758
John Singleton Copley (1738–1815), Medford, Massachusetts

I've made the Royall girls look that, indeed,
in gowns of Prussian blue and silver-gold.
To me their youthful beauty does not need
silk gowns, nor what their father has them hold—
a rare pet bird and a spaniel (King Charles),
as marks of wealth and Anglophile taste.
With Loyalist connections, Royall snarls
at me for painting Sam Adams. In haste
I say I take no view of Adams, and choose,
as well, to ignore the beleaguered slaves
in Royall's house; I can't afford to lose
a plum commission such as this. What saves
my hide is acting gentlemanly bland,
while giving what these wealthy men demand.

Charming Nelly

Miss Nelly O'Brien, circa 1762–1764
Sir Joshua Reynolds (1723–1792), London

Though Nelly O'Brien is a courtesan,
she sits for me with ease and confidence.
Society winks at Nelly and her man,
the Viscount keeping her at great expense.
He recklessly commissioned me to paint her
concurrent with a portrait of his *wife*.
Though *she's* unfaithful, too, I would not fault her,
or him, or Miss O'Brien—they chose that life.
I schedule sittings with the utmost care;
the work is going well. I find that Nelly's
warm and most attractive. Her candid stare
unnerves: as we converse my knees are jelly.
I paint the fluffy dog that's in her lap . . .
would that I could nestle like that chap.

Reflection

Old Woman Sitting, undated
Françoise Duparc (Spain, 1726–1778), location unknown

A washerwoman sits for me today.
Accepting francs, she says she's pleased to rest.
To answer why I chose her, I only say
the reddened arms she crosses at her breast
will frame her face that's washed in winter light.
The fichu round her neck is striped with blue;
from years of wear, that fabric's nearly white.
She seems to know that she is fading, too.
But with her gray-green, deep-set eyes that gaze
with quiet equanimity, she'll need
no painted flourishes or sweetened praise
from me. This woman's portrait may succeed
if viewers can perceive a will to live,
yet resignation for what fate will give.

Before the Revolution

Marie Antoinette in a Chemise Dress, 1783
Élisabeth Louise Vignée LeBrun (1755–1842)
Versailles, France

Portraying rich or royal in natural pose
and warm tones to flatter, I used more wits
and savvy than each subject might suppose.
The French have paid me well for pretty portraits—
thirty of Marie Antoinette.
This one caused a scandal. Her chemise
and straw hat created a vignette
of how a queen should *not* be seen—at ease,
at home. She'd been derided by the masses
for spendthrift ways and haughty, foreign air.
Too soon, derision turned on upper classes
and giddy minions who consorted there.
Before the mobs of '89 I fled,
kept up commissions, and never lost my head.

Traitor

Portrait of a Youth in an Embroidered Vest, 1785
Marie-Victoire Lemoine (1754–1820), Paris

A countess educated this young slave,
Zamor, then rued what proved her own undoing.
The young boy learned the lessons that she gave,
and as he grew, his bold outlook was brewing.
This protégé made mention, while I painted
him in satin, how he read Rousseau.
He chattered that King Louis's court was tainted
with opulence that he'd himself forgo
if every citizen were "free and equal."
Amid ensuing strife that I detested,
I learned of this accounting's dreadful sequel:
Zamor informed, the countess was arrested,
and after time in prison—never seen—
the countess, I heard, met the guillotine.

Little Bird

Francis O. Watts with Bird, 1805
John Brewster, Jr. (1766–1854), Kennebunk, Maine

This young boy's parents came to me distraught:
from scarlet fever, both their daughters perished.
A portrait of their son, age three, was sought
from me, a neighbor, who knew full well they cherished
their surviving sprout. In slippered feet
and lacy gown, the little lad stood still
for me to paint him. Later I'd complete
the eerie trees, the twilit empty hills,
the bird he's holding, tethered, as it sings.
This is a symbol of mortality:
the moment the holder dies, the bird takes wing,
loosed from string. The soul ascends, flies free.
Young Francis does not know his string is frail;
for now, he loves this trilling nightingale.

Unspoken

Elizabeth Grant Bankson Beatty (Mrs. James Beatty)
and Her Daughter Susan, circa 1805
Joshua Johnson (circa 1763–circa 1826), Baltimore

I hold some history close, about my birth
and youth. In ads I wrote, *I've been self-taught,*
confronted obstacles to test my worth,
and am a genius. My shameless tout has brought
good income from my portrait work, and chased
away self-doubt.
             This client wanted shine—
white lace, glass beads, brass tacks—her wealth and taste
displayed. She asked if I would stay to dine
but I departed at the dinner bell,
making mention of my family waiting
(no slaves to cook for us). I'd never tell
the facts my clients might find devastating:
my father was white, my mother a black slave
who gave me strength and schooled me to behave.

Little Soldier

José Costa y Bonells, Called Pepito, circa 1810
Francisco Goya (1746–1828), Madrid

Pepito is no bold or cocksure boy
with his soldier's hat, his drum, his bayonet.
In satin suit, he leads his horse (a toy),
while the saucer eyes of this pretend cadet
mourn like mine. The French have just invaded
Spain; our king was forced to abdicate.
Loyal Spanish fighters are paraded
before Napoleon's gunners seal their fate.
I'm making drawings of the violence,
preparing a painting of epic scale.
In tandem, as a sort of self-defense,
I paint this to divert or to curtail
my horror. But let Pepito's downcast eyes
suggest war's woe, and our proud land's demise.

Miss Moore No More

Mrs. Charles Willson Peale (Hannah Moore), 1816
Charles Willson Peale (1741–1827), Philadelphia

Miss Hannah Moore agreed to be my wife
within a year of my second bride's demise.
Although she'd been a spinster all her life,
Hannah had the knack to empathize
with children, yet morally upraise
the mites. She helped me teach the young ones still
at home; the older eight had gone their ways.
(With my nightly aching to fulfill,
my flock of Peales had grown to sixteen offspring.)
Though Hannah said she'd never brook relations,
I hoped someday there'd come a softening
and I agreed to her negotiations.
In time, she let me lie in bed with her—
we'd spoon. I did my darndest not to stir.

Afresh

The Torn Hat, 1820
Thomas Sully (England, 1783–1872), Philadelphia

How patiently my young son sat, who knew
he might be scolded, having torn his hat.
And were his flaming cheeks a residue
of shame for harrying our backyard cat?
I didn't ask, just had the rascal pose
right then in rumpled clothes, his little face
in dappled sunlight like a shadowed rose.
And as I worked, I hoped the marketplace
would see the same appeal I could perceive.
My portrait sales of late had dropped away.
With seven children, I needed to achieve
success—to find a fresh approach. Portraying
winsome innocence in a girl or boy
would pay me twice. My dividend was joy.

My Calling

Stu-mick-o-súcks, or Buffalo Bull's Back Fat, Head Chief, Blood Tribe, 1832
George Catlin (1796–1872), in territory that is now New Mexico

This Blackfoot war chief of the northern plains
is clad in battle dress—a deerskin shirt
adorned with quills of porcupine and skeins
of hair from those he scalped. Do you assert,
like most, that every Indian is savage?
Not one has ever betrayed me, struck me a blow,
or pilfered a thing of mine. The tribes are ravaged
by what we westward settlers have bestowed:
smallpox, measles, alcohol. My calling
is painting hundreds in their tribal dress,
then selling my collection for installing
in a capital site. My ultimate success,
a tribute to the tribes' nobility,
has met—as yet—with futility.

A Certain Symmetry

The Fortune Teller, circa 1835
Adèle Kindt (1804–1884), Brussels

The heavy cloak around my friend conceals
her state. She doubts the tarot cards will show
the baby's fate: her trace of smile reveals
amusement. But she suggested this tableau,
this study of the two, for me to paint:
she so young, so fair, and ruffled in silk
to show the world she spends without constraint;
and the fortune teller—of a foreign ilk
and likely born to struggle on the fringe—
who frowns with worried eyes and wizened skin.
I paint the pair and add a sort of hinge
between the two women: black fabric in
the lady's cloak and the seer's hood would fit
to form the specter neither can outwit.

Scandal

Madame X, 1843–1844
John Singer Sargent (Italy, 1856–1925), Paris

At last, when she allowed me to depict her,
this married beauty linked to love affairs,
the critics brayed I'd broken every stricture:
her brazen stance, décolleté, her air
aloof—as if with scorn her head is turned
aside. She flaunts herself and yet withdraws—
self-preservation I as well have learned.
Beyond this daring portrait, did I cause
reproof for what in me I must conceal?
Despite the furor, I didn't take this out
of public view. The work is vital, real—
and over time, its scandal gave me clout:
what once made Paris critics blanch and fret
now flaunts its beauty at the New York Met.

The Desperate Man

Le Désespéré, circa 1843–1845
Gustave Courbet (1819–1877), Paris

Bursting from the canvas, crazed, I stare;
I want to startle you and make you share
the pull of hands clawing through your hair.
No other painter shocks with equal flair
or paints so starkly only what is there.
The others want to prettify; I dare
to paint the truth. But yet I am aware
my path has risk. Last night I had a nightmare:
abandoned in a castle in the air.
I follow no salon, no standard-bearer,
have only the occasional affair.
With alternating fervor and despair,
I am alone. Tonight I am in terror
Courbet won't be remembered anywhere.

Arrangement, with Mother

Arrangement in Gray and Black No. 1
(also known as *Whistler's Mother*), 1871
James McNeill Whistler (United States, 1834–1903), London

I've placed my mother sideways in a space
composed of neutral shapes in two dimensions.
She's plainly angled, in widow's black; her face
is stern and slightly tilted down. Inventions
at my easel elevate my life;
the critics are approving of my art.
I cringe when Mother chides, "Find a wife,"
or worse, "Come home and make another start."
My mother cannot tell me what to do,
although her help lets me keep working on.
What sets her firmly on her judgment seat?
The pedestal I placed beneath her feet.
My mother might appear a paragon
or just another polygon to view.

Vows

The Cradle, 1872
Berthe Morisot (1841–1895), Paris

My sister sat beside the cradle, her gaze
intent upon her sleeping newborn daughter.
Critics give this painting passing praise—
"graceful, airy"—unaware I'd caught her
restless, searching in her artist's mind.
Those heady years! We'd learned to paint together,
with tutors, the Louvre a trove where we would find
new treasures every open hour, whether
chaperoned or not. Now, sacrifice:
my sister wishes painting could augment
her days, but family duties must suffice.
I posed her here inside a sort of tent
between the cradle net and window curtain—
a tent that makes a woman's art uncertain.

The Opera Box

In the Loge, 1878
Mary Cassatt (United States, 1844–1926), Paris

Leaning forward at the opera house,
this woman sits alone at a matinée.
To attend at night she'd need to have a spouse,
a father, brother, would-be fiancé . . .
ridiculous convention! Of youngish age
and modest dress, her bearing speaks of brains;
she rivets her attention on the stage.
Has she seen the distant man who trains
his gaze on her? His opera glasses peer
left as avidly as hers do straight ahead.
Left and right, the sight lines veer,
and then to you, it must be said—
so you are spying, too. Her only view
is art. She determines what she'll do.

My Present

Self-Portrait without Beard, 1889
Vincent van Gogh (Netherlands, 1853–1890)
Saint-Paul-de-Mausole Asylum, Saint-Rémy-de-Provence, France

Dearest Mother,
                I've painted this for you—
without my beard, I think you'll like me better.
My doctor says my thoughts are mostly true.
To him, to Theo, to you, I am a debtor.
I know my paltry sales can't be ignored.
I know with alcohol and sin I've failed
to follow all the teachings of our Lord.
I know that in my "episodes" I've railed
unfairly at my friends. But now I feel
a steadying, a turn. I've gained some weight
on decent food, and lately, by appeal,
they've let me paint. Thank God I can create.
I'm hoping that quite soon I will walk out,
restored to health, and almost free of doubt.

Allow Me to Present Myself

Self-Portrait from L'ile Saint Louis, 1890
Henri Rousseau (1844–1910), Paris

Remember me, this little man who stands
before you, brush and palette in his hands,
clad in his best suit and black beret.
This work proposes I am here to stay
beside the Eiffel Tower, boats, the Seine.
I aim to take my place with other men
trained in art, well connected, known.
This new pictorial style is mine alone;
primitive, critics dub it in derision.
It's true I shun the classic, mannered vision;
I shun, as well, the louche French artist's life.
A widower with children, I need a wife.
By day I am a tax collector; at night,
alone, I dream myself a leading light.

My First Tahitian Wife

Faaturuma (Melancholic), 1891
Paul Gauguin (France, 1848–1903), Tahiti

I watched this girl bathing in the river—
lithe of limb, copper skinned, black haired.
To learn her age (thirteen) gave me a shiver;
I quickly paid for her, and we were paired.
Tahitian women, missionaries say,
should cover up in dresses such as this
of billowed folds in shadowed rose. Today
my young vahine's quiet. Does she miss
the wild island life before the church
made staid monogamy the status quo?
I left a wife and children in the lurch
in France, but my new bride will never know.
And even if she did, I doubt she'd care—
these people understand how passions flare.

Incandescence

Flaming June, 1895
Sir Frederic Leighton (1830–1896), London

Does she, in gossamer orange, electrify
your senses? Do you hear her dreaming sighs—
or your intake of breath, as if you spy
a sight you should not see? Your widened eyes
will glide from face to hair to arms to thighs.
One long and lissome thigh intensifies
my own remembered want to gratify,
be one with this exotic butterfly
of June. She sleeps beside a pewter sky
and late-day golden water; evening's nigh.
Each day, each season, each of us, must die.
As I grow old, may this work signify
what I have learned too late: a firefly's
bright light is brief, and love may pass you by.

The Blue Hour

Summer Evening at Skagen Beach—the Artist and his Wife, 1899
Peder Severin Krøyer (1851–1909), Skagen, Denmark

At dusk the air would lure us out to stroll
the village beach, where sky and sea would mesh,
softly stitched into a fleeting whole.
The wholeness that was ours, of hearts and flesh,
was temporary, too. At times my mind
would send me to the hospital. Unhinged
or well, I found that friends and art would bind
my life to hope. My mental state infringed
on my much younger, lovely wife; she traveled
on her own, found another man,
and asked for a divorce. My world unraveled
even further when my sight began
to dim. Until I could no longer see,
I painted with what light was left in me.

On the Island

Portrait of Elizabeth, 1901
Frank Weston Benson (1862–1951), North Haven, Maine

Here at our summer home the day is fine.
The salty air's awash in light that she
reflects as she reflects on turning nine.
My daughter stands in sweet gentility—
her linen blouse with collar starched and bright,
a white to match the satin bow that ties
her honey hair. She makes a charming sight,
though shadow falls along her face. She sighs
and drops a pensive gaze on down our hill
to somewhere out beyond the sea-lapped shore.
Do nascent hopes and aspirations fill
her head? Is there some fear she can't ignore?
As she grows up this century, I pray
the world will be as peaceful as this day.

Stanislawa's Hair Is Brushed and Bowed

Self-Portrait with Daughter, 1907
Aniela Pajakówna (Poland, 1864–1912), location unknown

I'm painting worry in my shadowed eyes,
my careless hair, and how my mouth is set.
My daughter knows our state. She's six, and wise
beyond her years. Although she's hardly met
her father, Stani has his stalwart will
and clever mind. A budding dramatist,
she makes up lively stories while I fill
our trunks to move again. I'll never miss
Vienna, Krakow, Munich, Zurich: whispers,
tsking, turning shoulders. Paris is next.
I'll find a room for us that's near my sister.
Can't an artist ever earn respect
if she's a mother who has never wed?
Is there no more about her to be said?

To My Art Students

Patience Serious, 1915
Robert Henri (1865–1929), New York

My father killed a man. Our Midwest town
was named for Pa; there, I'd never shake
ignominy. I changed my name and found
my way to Paris, to study art and make
myself a different life. You all must dare
to break away like that. Ignore the sneers
of Design Academy muck-a-mucks. Share
your paintings with a few like-minded peers,
with eyes as sharp as this young moppet's gaze
of big brown eyes. Don't try to win acclaim.
Use painting to enlighten and amaze.
The means of making a living is not the same
as the means of living a life. If it is art
that spurs you on, you'll live a life with heart.

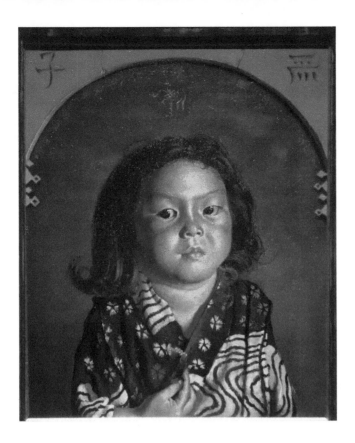

Devotion

Reiko, Five Years Old, 1918
Ryūsei Kishida (1891–1929), Fujisawa

I'm proud Japan supports the Allies' fight
as war in Europe staggers on in slaughter.
I find some peace in painting my young daughter.
Her apple cheeks glow in late-day light;
she's a beacon, shining through the murk
of olive green. I bless her with a red-
orange arch like a temple overhead.
I place her hand, as in religious work
that I admire, pointing toward her heart.
My cherub holds a tiny, bright-pink string
of lady's thumb as if a sacred thing—
a common weed, but still a work of art.
It's art to sanctify not Buddha or Christ,
but all young lives the war has sacrificed.

After Influenza

Self-Portrait after the Spanish Flu, 1919
Edvard Munch (1863–1944), Oslo

Painting quickly, still a little weak
from my abysmal bout with Spanish flu,
I stare with baggy, bleary eyes. I streak
a bilious green around my mouth, gray-blue
along my jaw, vermillion over brows
(the fire of my fever), and a brown dent
centered in forehead—a stigma that avows
my guilt, recovering from this event.
My mental health has never been robust
and I am nearing sixty; what right have I
to live? What kind of God would entrust
health to me while letting millions die
when in their prime? I can only pray
this menace will not strike another day.

On My Terms

Portrait of Jeanne Hébuterne, 1919
Amedeo Modigliani (Italy, 1884–1920), Paris

I rarely make a sale, but still I strike
my mark in artists' circles. Everyone knows
I drink and smoke hashish. Sometimes I like
stripping off my clothes at parties. I chose
to leave behind my bourgeois youth; the route
to real art is disorder and defiance.
Although I am unwell and destitute,
I seek no help and I reject alliance
with any group or style. Still, I'm tied
to sweet and gentle Jeanne—she's expecting
soon, and we're engaged. She's terrified
TB is claiming me. But self-protecting
is not my game. A fierce brevity
dances on the grave of tame longevity.

Brood

House of Cards, 1919
Zinaida Serebriakova (Ukraine, 1884–1967), location unknown

No chatter from these four, nor a smile.
My children build a house of cards to while
away an afternoon. Their listless eyes
reflect cascading loss and compromise.
Their Papa died, imprisoned without cause
by Bolsheviks who scoffed at Russian laws.
They looted and burned our beloved country home.
I paint my children in a monochrome
(I found an unused tube of Prussian blue);
we face the choice of decent, healthy food
or oil paints. I'll start next week to sketch
with cheaper charcoal on paper. I will fetch
what cash I can, and work with speed and prayer.
This painting holds my love and my despair.

When I Was Young

Untitled (Self-Portrait), 1924–1925
Emily Carr (1871–1945), Victoria, British Columbia

I liked my mop of chestnut hair cropped short.
No need to brush before I'd rush outside
to the woodland park nearby, where I'd consort
with creatures blessedly undignified.
A wren or rabbit wouldn't have to hear
"Mop up your muddy footprints yet again . . .
girls are judged by how they first appear . . .
of course you'll marry. All girls do, when
they reach a certain age . . . now do your chores
and learn another Bible verse today."
My father ruled. On rainy days, indoors,
I'd sketch or paint. Just once I heard him say,
"You do not act the way a daughter should,
but my dear Em, your artist's eye is good."

My Other Life

I and My Model, 1929–1930
Lotte Laserstein (1898–1993), Berlin

In the twenties, before the Brown Shirts' rise,
a woman like me could live almost as free
as a man. We seldom saw chastising eyes
when walking arm in arm, my model and me.
Rose was slim and striking, and she was bolder,
tougher. Here she stands in just a slip
and rests a hand lightly on my shoulder.
Then came the tightened screws of Nazi grip,
and Jewish artists weren't allowed to show
their work or even buy supplies. Escaping
to Sweden, I wept that Rose refused to go.
I'm drawing children's portraits now, and scraping
by. This work I keep recalls the time—
how could I know it then?—that was my prime.

Lifelines

Portrait of Beauford Delaney, 1943, pastel
Georgia O'Keeffe (1887–1986), New York

I know he's troubled, this quiet, well-dressed man.
Although the critics praise Delaney's art,
it doesn't sell. He earns what cash he can
posing for other artists like me, and part-
time work as doorman or museum guard.
He hints at liking men; that's not at rights
with Christian precepts he was taught. "So hard,"
he shakes his head, "to live by my own lights."
He murmurs he's afraid he'll come unstrung.
I've come unstrung myself, with my depression
and a breakdown. Each of us has clung
to painting as our refuge and obsession.
We wrestle with our objects of devotion—
a burning bush, a bone, the wide sky-ocean.

You Will Remember Me

The Broken Column, 1944
Frida Kahlo (1907–1954), Mexico City

Does it make you gasp to see this fissure
in my naked torso, revealing pieces
of my shattered spine? No surgeon's scissor,
plaster cast, or corset ever decreases
constant pain, as if I had been nailed
like this. My trunk is buckled up in straps—
supports that shorten every breath inhaled.
Polio and accident have trapped
me in a body crisscrossed by ravines.
Across my stoic face a dozen tears
are scattered pearls. I've made quite a scene,
in art and life; I've done that all these years.
Between these straps my breasts bulge out like eyes.
Don't I look a strange and sexual prize?

My Brother with the Same Name

Portrait of My Dead Brother, 1963
Salvador Dalí (1904–1989), Cadaqués, Spain

Growing up, the bane of my existence
was being made the stand-in for my brother.
That Salvador succumbed, age one; the *Persistence
of Memory* was wound around my mother.

At seven, I wanted to be Napoleon,
and my ambition's been growing ever since.
May each Moroccan and Mongolian
know my name as art's eccentric prince.

I drape my cape and wax my curled mustache . . .
I drove my Rolls in that cauliflower caper . . .
I pissed on Warhol's artwork . . . with panache.
It made him laugh! *Mamá* would get the vapors.

In time I'm certain that my fame will make
that brother ancient myth, for *my* name's sake.

I Didn't Mean to Tell You That

Reflection with Two Children (Self-Portrait), 1965
Lucian Freud (Germany, 1922–2011), London

Hello below, you lowly gallery viewers
down beside the mirror at my feet.
This novel angle, I assume, skewers
what you might think of me: *What conceit!*
Freud's posturing to pump his ego. Agreed!
But do admire my design in gray
and these tiny, perfect tots of the lot I breed.
I'd celebrate an Unwed Mother's Day
(libido and bravado serve me well).
Of course, my wives have left. I'd leave me, too.
I left behind my childhood, impelled
to flee from prewar Germany, a Jew
who tried and failed to join the Hitler youth.
I never did fit in, and that's the truth.

Mother and Child

Mother and Child (Nancy and Olivia), 1967
Alice Neel (1900–1984), New York

Portrait painting, so long out of fashion,
was all I did. Not by commission—I'd ask
a friend whose face was lined by life and passion
to sit. Then I'd distort a bit: a mask
would simplify and heighten the emotion.
My daughter-in-law's eyes are spelling fear
as she holds her baby tightly with devotion,
for protection from who could appear
through that open door. I told my story,
how my husband stole our second daughter
and fled the country. I told, as well, the gory
gist of losing our firstborn. I caught her
terror as she sat, and watched it spread
into her baby's eyes, as fixed as dead.

Out of Sight

Julia Warhola, 1974, mixed media
Andy Warhol (1928–1987), New York

My mother's great, but *she doesn't get out of bed*
much. That's how I answer those who ask;
I leave her death, a few years back, unsaid.
My bit of gallows humor serves to mask
my grieving. I recall my mother's care
for me, a sickly kid (and quirky, odd);
her saintly patience, floating daily prayers
"for Andy's health and happiness" to God;
her moving to New York to live with me
(flat broke); assisting me for twenty years,
selflessly, until her late seventies.
I'm well aware of how it would appear—
my absence at my mother's funeral rite.
I only cope when death is out of sight.

Dear Mum,

Imperial Nude (Paul Rosano), 1977
Sylvia Sleigh (Wales, 1916–2010), New York

Just got your letter and the clipping. I see
your local critic's "utterly appalled"
by this, my latest painting, and you agree.
Mum, why so shocked to see a guy who's sprawled
across a couch and happens to be nude?
Think of Goya, Rubens, Ingres, Renoir—
the Old Masters hardly thought it rude
to paint idealized, naked *women*. Men are
handsome individuals; God knows
I never try to paint an archetype.
I'm proud my work's in several New York shows,
so screw the *Welsh Gazette*, Mum. Don't snipe
about appearances—forget all that.
I pay this model, paint him, and we chat.

Helga

Overflow, 1978
Andrew Wyeth (1917–2009), Chadds Ford, Pennsylvania

I didn't paint our neighbor Helga *naked*—
that connotes embarrassed, stripped, or cold.
I'd call her *bare*—instinctive, somehow sacred.
Her strong and supple body would unfold
and lie in perfect peace and natural ease,
wherever. She's lying on an attic bed
here, on an August night. A whiff of breeze
came through to brush her hips and back and head;
she smiled slightly as she held the pose.
For fifteen years I learned beside this muse,
as if some inner truth had shed its clothes
and led my brush to paint my finest views.
Was she my lover? That I will not say.
This is an ode, and not an exposé.

What Do They Know?

Versus Medici, 1982, mixed media
Jean-Michel Basquiat (1960–1988), New York

One critic wrote, "His career is a hoax . . .
its marketing pure baloney." Now the joke's
on him, as there's no lack of loaded folks
snapping up my works. This one pokes
the ribs of history's old-boned, white elite—
I'm saying it's Medicis I unseat!
I'm Black, untrained, and young—but I compete.
I started with graffiti, on the street
a couple years. I'd scrounge, panhandle, steal,
and hustle, turning on the sex appeal.
Then clubbing led to shows . . . and *boom for real.*
Now I work nonstop. It's no big deal
I'm heavy into weed and smack and coke—
but Basquiat will not go up in smoke.

Boterismo

The Poet, 1987
Fernando Botero (b. 1932), Medellín

I paint a pudgy poet in a glade.
He's beefy and he's hungry for the lines
to polish off a sonnet to serenade
his love. His tie's askew as he reclines
beside his paper, scribbling put aside.
He stares out from the canvas and he broods;
the muse has flown. He's moonfaced, beady eyed,
desperate for the opus that eludes
him. Maybe I can help him in his courtship:
I'll paint more peaches dropping from the trees;
he'll hold one in his chubby-fingered grip.
"So sweet," he'll murmur, giving it a squeeze,
imagining his luscious ingénue.
Soon words will fall on him with which to woo.

Close-Up

Self-Portrait, 2000
Chuck Close (1940–2021), New York

I'm in my wheelchair, a brush strapped to my wrist.
It's more than twenty years since *The Event*,
the stroke that locked my hand into a fist.
But my persistence made me reinvent
my style. High-chroma color is now profuse:
abstract up close, but a realistic face
emerges from my splotches, dots, and loose
grid, when looked at from a farther place.
Your normal brain and eyes complete the picture.
As I work I don't move back to view it
for likeness. If that comes, it's from the stricture
of grid and dots. Slow work. But as I do it,
lacking facial recognition, my brain
and eyes work with the grid, connect a chain.

Black Bird

Self-Portrait: Black Bird, 2002
Julie Dowling (b. 1969), Perth

My clan's creature, the wedge-tailed eagle, black,
outspreads imperfect wings across my chest.
I paint its silhouette to bring me back
clear through what I have written on my dress—
First Nation names; the eagle carries me
into the bush and to my proud, deep roots
in Badimaya country. My enmity
flares at White police who persecute
our groups. Their agents used to steal some light-
skinned kids from First Nation families
and place them in church missions or with Whites.
With a pair of fair-skinned daughters men could seize,
my mother kept us on the run. I flew.
My paintings bring my people into view.

Tell Me What You Think

They Call Me Redbone but I'd Rather Be Strawberry Shortcake, 2009
Amy Sherald (b. 1973), Baltimore

My private school classmates called me "Redbone,"
southern slang for a Black with lighter skin.
It didn't offend me, much. With a White voice tone,
the right clothes and hair, I almost fit in.
My schoolgirl head is cocked to one side here
as if to ask my viewers what they think.
Your preconceptions might just disappear
if you survey my work. I break the link
with past portrait painters (read: White men),
since I don't show a sitter's social standing
or character by painting in, for him
or her or them, a context. I'm demanding
you consider common notions of race
and the thoughts behind each Black subject's face.

Imagining Caleb

Caleb Cheeshahteaumuck, 2010
Stephen E. Coit (b. 1948), Cambridge, Massachusetts

So very few at Harvard looked like him
back then—his skin nut-brown, hair straight and black.
I picture this young man stern and grim,
yet proud in academic gown. At his back
is a map of Martha's Vineyard he likely drew,
his island home. He must have felt defined
by autumn harvest feasts, by hunts on snowshoes,
spring herring runs, and summer berry wine.
Did Caleb plan that someday he'd return
and, like his father, be a chief? Would one
so learned, schooled in church and classics, earn
respect or scorn in the tribe where he'd begun?
He never knew. He took a room near here,
and perished of TB within the year.

Afterword

ARE THESE POEMS FACT OR FICTION? Historical fiction, I'd say. These persona poems (in which the poet speaks through an assumed voice) are based on research in books and online sources, as well my imagination and interpretation. I tried to suggest the artist's "voice" (vocabulary and tone) along with the thoughts or life story he or she might choose to reveal. Sometimes I felt like a detective, uncovering clues that led me to my own conclusions about the paintings and the artists.

Ideally, every poem would appear with a color reproduction of the painting referenced. Wikimedia Commons has been a wonderful source of public domain images of all the older works, but obtaining permission to reprint modern artworks is a complex and expensive process. It is easy, however, to find the absent images online. There are directions for online searches in "Notes," beginning on page 71.

My own art background informed this collection. My degree from Skidmore College was in studio art, and I was a professional artist for about forty years, first in graphic design and then in art quilts. I wrote these poems during the COVID-19 pandemic, and I marvel at the way artists throughout history have worked through similar pandemics, as well as wars, poverty, discrimination, physical or mental illness, and every other sort of upheaval or difficulty—with or without public recognition of their work. Researching and writing about these artists has sustained and inspired me. This book is written in tribute to them.

I am grateful to the members of the Powow River Poets workshop, especially to Jean L. Kreiling, for helpful suggestions with these poems. Editor Alex Pepple has been absolutely stellar; I thank him enormously for his perspicacity and patience. And as always, I thank my husband, Bill, for his steadiness and good humor.

B.L.C.
Somerville, Massachusetts
February 13, 2023

"Marie de Valengin" on page 3: Philip the Good, the duke of Burgundy, did bring his illegitimate daughter Marie to live with him at court, but I am imagining what she confides to the artist here.

"A Painting for Private Devotion" on page 4: Mantegna was the first in northern Italy to be widely recognized as a Renaissance painter.

"Rivals" on page 8: Raphael is referring to his archrival, Michelangelo, and that artist's famed sculpture *David*.

"The Old Commander" on page 10: What this commander did was considered honorable in this time and place; indeed, it was thought to be the duty of a son or younger brother to avenge the murder of his father or older brother. This practice was made illegal in Japan in 1873.

"The Miniaturist" on page 12: Teerlinc worked at the English courts of Henry VIII, Edward VI, Mary I, and Elizabeth I.

"Arrangements" on page 13: Fontana's arranged marriage was to Gian Zappi, a minor painter who gave up his career and became her agent and assistant—choices that were practically unheard of in Italy at that time.

"No Angels" on page 15: *Death of the Virgin* was rejected by Caravaggio's patron, a papal legal advisor, who may or may not have known this prostitute. But Caravaggio did.

"The Poem I Tucked into the Frame" on page 16: It's thought by some scholars that after van Mierevelt's wife died, he painted her image into an existing self-portrait.

"Presenting Myself" on page 18: Judith Leyster was probably the first female painter admitted to the Haarlem Guild. Until 1893 all her works were mistakenly attributed to Franz Hals or to her husband, Jan Molenaar.

"What I Tell Myself" on page 19: Molenaar was not as financially successful as his wife, Judith Leyster.

"Girl with a Turban" on page 21: *Girl with a Turban* was this painting's original title. One of Vermeer's daughters may have been his model for it.

"The Empty Lap of Luxury" on page 22: No one knows why this painting was left incomplete, but this poem presents my theory. Gainsborough was struggling financially, and by some accounts he was resentful of this wealthy young couple. Perhaps he refused to paint the genteel flowers or book that the couple might have requested to fill Mrs. Andrews' lap. Since Mr. Andrews was a hunter, Gainsborough may have suggested, instead, a fresh-killed bird—phrased differently. Since the artist reportedly had a bawdy sense of humor, I like to think he'd get a hearty laugh from my last line.

"Royall Treatment" on page 23: I'm taking some liberties here with dates. Copley did paint Sam Adams, but it was not until the 1760s that Adams became a heated proponent for colonial freedom from Britain. Isaac Royall, in what is now Medford, Massachusetts, owned a dozen Black slaves.

"Reflection" on page 25: Very little is known about Françoise Duparc; the story behind this painting is imagined.

"Traitor" on page 27: Zamor was a Bengali boy kidnapped by British slave traders and sold to the king of France, who gave the boy to his mistress, a countess. In the French Revolution Zamor sided with the Jacobins and reported the countess to the Committee of Public Safety; her arrest and subsequent death ensued. Zamor was briefly imprisoned himself. In later life he was a teacher and died in poverty.

"Unspoken" on page 29: Johnson placed this self-advertisement in the *Baltimore Intelligencer* of 19 December 1798, which currently appears online (scroll down) at: "Face to Face," the *Magazine ANTIQUES*, 13 September 2021, www.themagazineantiques.com/article/face-to-face/, accessed 28 January 2023.

"Little Soldier" on page 30: France invaded Spain in 1808 and governed there until 1814. The epic work in progress that Goya mentions is *The Third of May, 1808*, considered by many the greatest antiwar painting ever made.

"My Calling" on page 33: In 1879, seven years after Catlin's death, the entire collection that he called "Indian Gallery" was given by a benefactor to the Smithsonian Museum in Washington, DC, where it remains, in the Renwick Gallery. The artist is paraphrased in lines 6 and 7 from Bruce Watson, "George Catlin's Obsession," *Smithsonian Magazine*, December 2002, www.smithsonianmag.com/arts-culture/george-catlins-obsession-72840046/.

"A Certain Symmetry" on page 34: I've imagined the story and Adèle Kindt's intent, based on my own interpretation of the painting.

"Arrangement, with Mother" on page 37: Apparently Whistler feared disapproval: he had his girlfriend move out just before his mother's arrival. His mother lived with him, keeping house and helping manage his business affairs, from 1864 to 1875. Whistler married in 1888.

"Vows" on page 38: Two years after painting this, Morisot entered an arranged marriage, giving her societal position and financial security. Her husband, a brother of the artist Édouard Manet, gave up his own painting career so that Morisot could continue hers; they had one child, a daughter.

"My Present" on page 40: Van Gogh was pronounced "cured" and released from the Saint-Rémy Asylum shortly after painting this self-portrait. Just two months later he died of a gunshot wound, more than likely self-inflicted.

"Incandescence" on page 43: Leighton and his model may have been the prototypes for George Bernard Shaw's play *Pygmalion*. Leighton educated Dorothy Dene (born Ada Pullen) and introduced her to society. Though they sometimes traveled together, it's not known if they were intimate. Leighton never married.

"On the Island" on page 45: For the artwork, go to this digital archive: arthur.io/art/frank-weston-benson/portrait-of-elizabeth/.

"Stanislawa's Hair Is Brushed and Bowed" on page 46: Pajakówna had a brief affair with Stanislaw Przybyszewski, a Polish dramatist and poet. Pajakówna died of pneumonia five years after painting this, and her daughter was then cared for by an aunt in Paris. The daughter became a playwright, like her father.

"To My Art Students" on page 47: The artist is paraphrased often from Robert Henri, *The Art Spirit*, Harper & Row, 1923.

"When I Was Young" on page 52: Some sources mention Carr's "big reveal" (her term) in a talk she had with her father when she was about fifteen. She never divulged the subject of this talk; my own guess is that she said she never intended to marry. Carr did remain single.

"My Other Life" on page 53: This artwork is not so easy to find. Search for "Lotte Laserstein, Ich und mein Modell" or go to https://www.tagblatt.ch/kultur/kunstkolumne-bildbetrachtung-von-sabine-altorfer-diese-woche-d Yes ie-malerin-und-ihr-emanzipiertes-modell-ld.2210165?reduced=true.

"Lifelines" on page 54: For an image of the Georgia O'Keeffe artwork, search online for "National Portrait Gallery, Beauford Delaney," or go to https://npg.si.edu/object/npg_NPG.2002.1/.

"You Will Remember Me" on page 55: Kahlo was born with spina bifida, contracted polio at age six, was in a near-fatal bus accident at age eighteen, and underwent thirty-two subsequent operations in attempts to repair her spine from that accident.

"My Brother with the Same Name" on page 56: Dalí's parents considered him the reincarnation of his deceased brother, the first Salvador, and his mother often took him to his brother's gravesite. *The Persistence of Memory* is Dalí's famous painting of 1931, with clocks that appear to be melting and a grotesque, vaguely human shape in the center. For the artwork, search online for "Portrait of My Dead Brother." The artist is quoted in line 5 and paraphrased in line 6 from the *Dalí Universe*, "Salvador Dalí Quotes," www.thedaliuniverse.com/en/salvador-dali/quotes/, accessed 28 January 2023.

"I Didn't Mean to Tell You That" on page 57: Grandson of Sigmund Freud (with whom he had a good relationship, though he denied that his artwork was influenced by psychiatry), Lucian Freud was possibly bisexual and reportedly a misogynist. He was divorced three times, had many mistresses, and had several children both in and out of marriage (he acknowledged fourteen). For the artwork, search online for "Reflection with Two Children (Self-Portrait)."

"Out of Sight" on page 59: For an image of the artwork, search online for "Julia Warhola, 1974," or go to https://revolverwarholgallery.com/julia-warhola-artist-mother-king-pop-art/. The artist is paraphrased and quoted at the start of the poem from "Sons, Mothers, and Lovers," *Artforum*, May 2017, www.artforum.com/print/201705/ara-osterweil-on-andy-warhol-s-and-rainer-werner-fassbinder-s-queer-home-movies-67936/, accessed 28 January 2023.

"Dear Mum," on page 60: For the artwork, search online for "Sylvia Sleigh, Imperial Nude (Paul Rosano)," or go to https://news.artnet.com/art-world/ great-women-artists-book-1706142/ (scroll down).

"What Do They Know?" on page 62: Art critic Hilton Kramer did say these things, paraphrased here from a 1985 *New York Observer* review. "Boom for real" was Basquiat's phrase, meaning using everything that inspired him and making it all "explode onto the canvas." He died of a drug overdose at age twenty-seven. For the artwork, search online for "Versus Medici."

"Boterismo" on page 63: "Boterismo" is this artist's signature style of depicting obese people cartoonishly, for political commentary or for humor. I've imagined the story of the poem.

"Close-Up" on page 64: In 1988 Close suffered "The Event" (his term), a sudden rupture of his spinal artery; he recovered only partial use of his limbs. He also had severe dyslexia and prosopagnosia (the inability to recognize faces). For the artwork, search online for "Chuck Close Self-Portrait 2000."

"Imagining Caleb" on page 67: In 1665, Caleb Cheeshahteaumuck was the first Native American to graduate from Harvard. He and his four Native American classmates were housed in a separate dormitory, called Indian College. Two died of disease, one died in a shipwreck, and one left school. This young man died of tuberculosis just months after graduating.

Barbara Lydecker Crane's poems have been widely published in formal-friendly journals and anthologies. Her previous poetry collections are *Zero Gravitas, AlphabeTricks* (for children), both published by Kelsay Books, and *Back Words Logic*, published by Local Gems Press. She loves writing and art making in equal measure, and also enjoys traveling, either solo or with her family.

CPSIA information can be obtained
at www.ICGtesting.com
Printed in the USA
JSHW040947250523
42210JS00003B/42